THE FIRST MORNING

A very long time ago, there was no sunlight in the world. It was hard for the animals to see anything at all.

They fell into holes.

They tripped over rocks.

They crashed into each other!

One day Lion called a meeting.
"We must have light," he said.
"When there is a thunderstorm,
a great light splits the sky. Who will
go and get some of that light?"

Mouse stepped forward. "I am only
small, but I will try," she said.

"And we will help you!" said Spider
and Fly.

The three small creatures worked out a plan. First of all, Spider spun a huge web that reached up to the clouds.

Then Mouse and Fly climbed up the web. Mouse nibbled a small hole in the sky, and they all crawled through it and out the other side.

The small creatures were amazed
to find a land on the other side.
And there, staring at them, was the
Sky King.

"What do you want here?"
boomed the King.

"Please," said Mouse, bowing low,
"we want to take some light back to
earth."

"It's dark down there," said Spider.

"And we all keep bumping into
each other!" said Fly.

At first the King did not reply.
Then he said, "I must ask my people."

But the King and his people did not want to share the light.

"Let's give those creatures a task to do before we give them light," said one of the Sky People.

"But make it too hard for them!" said another.

"I have a plan," said the King, and he called for Mouse and said, "We need grass to build new houses. If you cut enough grass for one hundred houses by tomorrow morning, we will give you light."

No one knew that Fly was listening to all this, too.

When Fly told Mouse and Spider what he had overheard, they were furious.

"They have all this light and don't want to share it!" said Spider.

"Now *we* must think of a cunning plan," said Mouse.

They decided that Spider would climb back down her web and ask the grasshoppers for help.

That night, all the grasshoppers climbed up through the hole in the sky. They cut enough grass to build one hundred houses. Then they hurried back down to earth.

The next morning, when the Sky King and his people saw that all the grass had been cut, they were astonished.

But they still did not want to share the light.

"I will set another task," said the King.

The King took the three friends into a huge room filled with different kinds of grain.

"Sort all this grain into separate piles of corn, wheat, and rice by the morning. Then I will give you light."

The King left, locking the door behind him. Fly flew out through a tiny hole in the wall and climbed down the web to earth. There he asked his friends, the ants, to come and help.

They sorted and sorted all night long, and in the morning there were separate piles of corn, wheat, and rice to show the King.

The King could not believe his eyes. He began to think that he *should* share the light with such clever creatures.

But he decided to set one final task. "They will have to choose between these two boxes," he told his people. "The yellow box holds darkness. The red box holds light."

No one knew that Fly was listening to all this, too.

Fly hurried back to Mouse and told her which box to choose.

When Mouse stood before the Sky King and his people, she pretended to think for a moment. Then she pointed to the red box.

"I choose this one," said Mouse, and she snatched the box and slid quickly down the web to earth.

Back on earth all the animals gathered around.

"Open the box," they all cried.

Ever so slowly, Mouse lifted the lid. A large bird stared back at her.

"This is not light!" roared Lion. "It is only a bird!"

Mouse hung her head in shame. She and her small friends had been tricked, after all.

But none of the animals knew that the bird was a rooster!

Suddenly the rooster jumped up.

Cock-a-doodle-doo, he crowed.

Cock-a-doodle-doo, he crowed again.

Cock-a-doodle-doo, he crowed for a third time, and golden light flooded the earth.

The rooster had called up the sun and brought the first morning.

And from that day to this, roosters call up the sun every day!